BIRDS
WINGED AND FEATHERED ANIMALS

by Suzanne Slade

illustrated by Kristin Kest

Picture Window Books
Minneapolis, Minnesota

Thanks to our advisers for their expertise, research, and advice:

Robert C. Dowler, Ph.D.
Tippett Professor of Biology
Angelo State University
San Angelo, Texas

Terry Flaherty, Ph.D., Professor of English
Minnesota State University, Mankato

Editor: Shelly Lyons
Designer: Lori Bye
Page Production: Melissa Kes
Art Director: Nathan Gassman
Editorial Director: Nick Healy
Creative Director: Joe Ewest
The illustrations in this book were created with oil paints.

Photo Credits: page 22 (top row, left to right, and repeated uses):
Shutterstock/Steve Byland, iStockphoto/Laure Neish,
Shutterstock/Gregg Williams, Shutterstock/Ron Waldrop,
iStockphoto/Julie Masson, iStockphoto/George Peters,
iStockphoto/Eric Isselee, Shutterstock/Paul-Andre
Belle-Isle, iStockphoto/Maxim Kulko, iStockphoto/Le Do.

Picture Window Books
151 Good Counsel Drive
P.O. Box 669
Mankato, MN 56002-0669
877-845-8392
www.picturewindowbooks.com

All books published by Picture Window Books
are manufactured with paper containing at least
10 percent postconsumer waste.

Library of Congress Cataloging-in-Publication Data
Slade, Suzanne.
Birds : winged and feathered animals / by Suzanne Slade ;
illustrated by Kristin Kest.
p. cm. — (Amazing science. Animal classification)
Includes index.
ISBN 978-1-4048-5522-9 (library binding)
1. Birds—Classification—Juvenile literature. 2. Birds—Juvenile literature.
I. Kest, Kristin, ill. II. Title
QL677.S58 2010
598—dc22   2009003289

TABLE OF CONTENTS

A World Full of Animals

Millions of animals live on our planet. Scientists classify animals, or group them together, by looking at how the animals are alike or different.

ostrich, emu, rhea

tinamou

owl

duck, goose, swan

turkey, chicken, pheasant

penguin

eagle, hawk, falco

Scientists have found about 10,000 different kinds of birds in the world. All birds have certain things in common: feathers and wings, a backbone, lightweight bones, and a four-chambered heart. They are warm-blooded, and they hatch from eggs.

Six of the more familiar main groups of animals living on Earth are: mammals, birds, reptiles, amphibians, fish, and insects. Let's take a closer look at birds.

hummingbird and swift

parrot

Passeriformes

heron

Feathers and Wings

All birds have feathers and wings. Feathers protect birds' skin from the sun and keep birds warm during winter. Feathers are also lightweight and help birds fly.

Most birds have strong wings and can fly fast and far. Many travel hundreds of miles each year when they migrate to new places.

ring-necked ducks

mallard ducks

Birds preen, or clean, their feathers often. They use their hard beaks to comb their feathers.

7

Bones and Blood

Every bird has a skeleton made of a backbone and other small bones inside its body. Animals with backbones are called vertebrates. Many bird bones have spaces of air in them. These light bones allow birds to fly better.

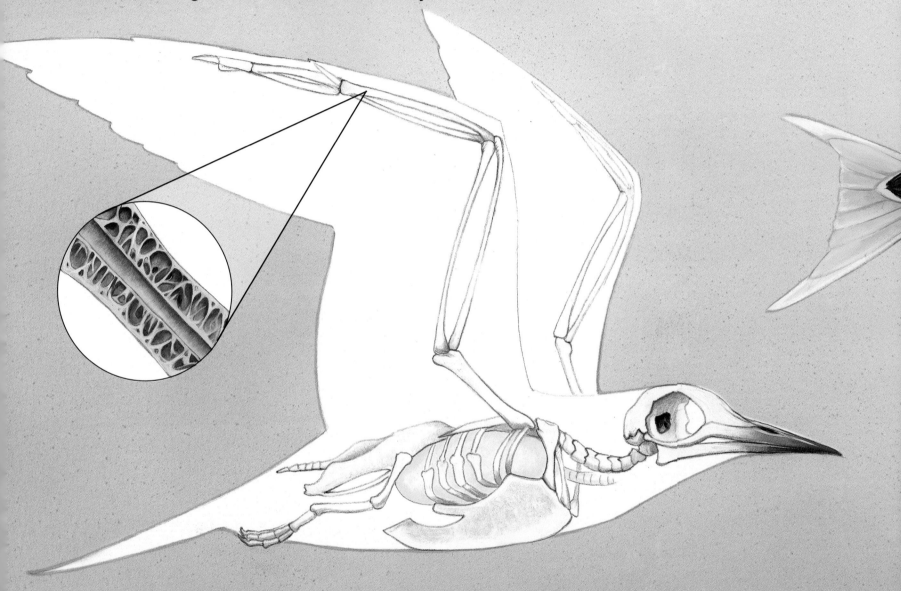

Birds have hearts with four chambers, or large spaces. They are also warm-blooded animals. That means their body temperature almost always stays the same.

Arctic terns

As they soar through the sky, birds breathe in a gas called oxygen with their lungs. Like people, birds need oxygen to live.

9

Beginning as an Egg

A bird's life begins inside an egg covered with a hard shell. Most female birds lay their eggs in nests. A parent bird often sits on the eggs to keep them safe and warm until the young birds hatch.

Parent birds bring food to their young until the young are old enough to leave the nest. Birds can fly a few weeks after hatching.

barn swallows

Most birds build their nests out of sticks, feathers, and grasses. But some do not. A small bird called a swallow uses mud and feathers to make its nest.

11

Home, Sweet Home

Birds live in different habitats all around the world. Many birds, such as colorful macaws and parrots, live in warm, sunny places.

macaw

Amazon parrot

The hot, dry desert is home to the singing cactus wren. Large roadrunners also love to sprint across the desert sand at speeds of about 17 miles (27.2 kilometers) per hour.

cactus wren

roadrunner

Perching and Water Birds

Robins, cardinals, and other perching birds live in woodlands and gardens. These birds have four strong toes that grip branches tightly. A perching bird does not fall off a branch when it sleeps because its toes keep squeezing as it snoozes.

cardinals

robins

Water birds live near lakes, rivers, and oceans. Most are graceful swimmers as well as strong fliers. Ducks, swans, and geese use their webbed feet to paddle on the water. Storks and flamingos have long, stick-like legs. They wade in shallow water and search for food.

wood duck

mallard duck

flamingo

Water birds have oil on their feathers to keep them dry. These waterproof feathers also help water birds stay warm.

15

Hungry Birds

Birds that hunt and kill other animals for food are called predators. Eagles and owls are predators. They have good eyesight and sharp claws to catch their prey. Vultures and other scavenger birds eat dead animals. Scavengers use their sense of smell to find food.

golden eagle

Many birds, such as peacocks and chickens, eat seeds and fruit. Some birds dine on insects and worms.

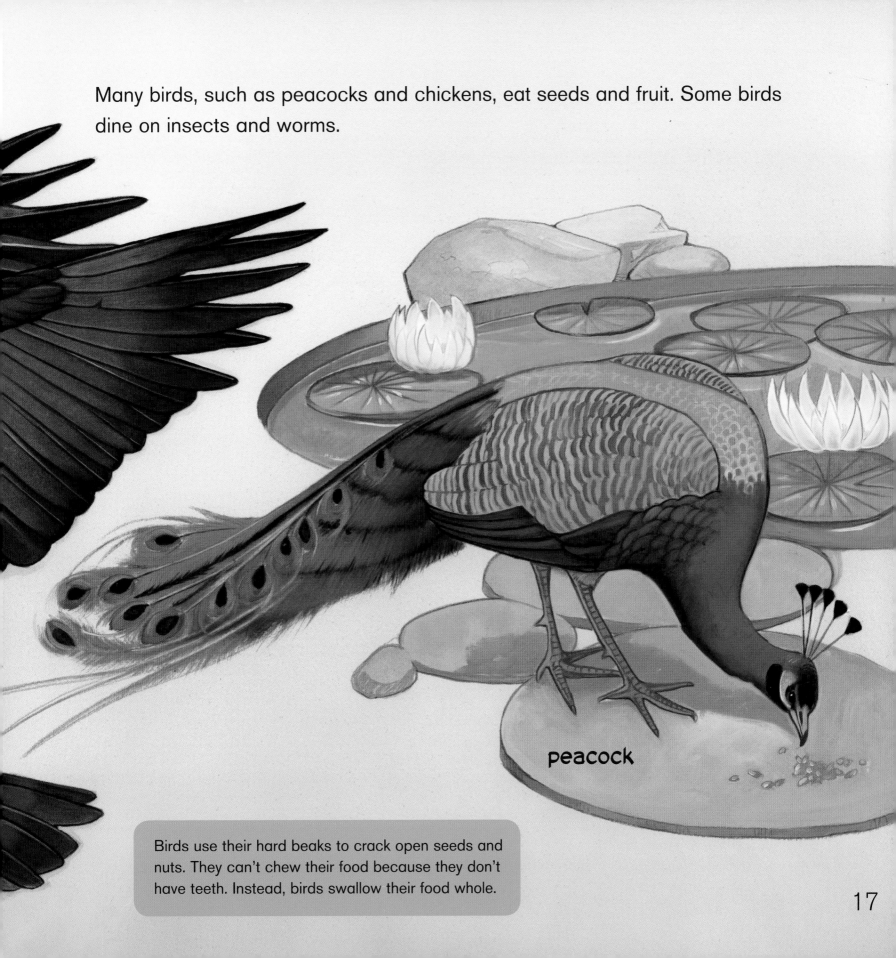

peacock

Birds use their hard beaks to crack open seeds and nuts. They can't chew their food because they don't have teeth. Instead, birds swallow their food whole.

Flightless Birds

All birds have wings, but not all birds can fly. Flightless birds have other ways of getting around. With their short legs, penguins waddle slowly across surfaces. In water, their wings work like flippers to help them swim fast.

emperor penguins

Ostriches and emus have long, strong legs for running. An ostrich can run as fast as 43 miles (68.8 kilometers) per hour!

ostriches

The dodo bird once lived on the island of Mauritius, but it was extinct by 1681. It had a chubby gray body and short legs. Although it had wings, it didn't use them to fly. It is known for its funny name and hooked beak.

Strange Birds

Swifts spend most of their lives in the air. They eat, mate, and even sleep while flying!
Bee eaters have an unusual diet. They often munch on bees and wasps.

bee eater

swift

20

Hummingbirds are amazing fliers. They can hover in one place and fly backward.

hummingbirds

Birds called cuckoos are not crazy, but they are pushy. Many cuckoos lay their eggs in other birds' nests. Once the young cuckoos hatch, they shove the other young birds out of the nest.

Scientific Classification Chart

The animal classification system used today was created by Carolus Linnaeus. The system works by sorting animals based on how they are alike or different.

All living things are first put into a kingdom. There are five main kingdoms. Then they are also assigned to groups within six other main headings. The headings are: phylum, class, order, family, genus, and species.

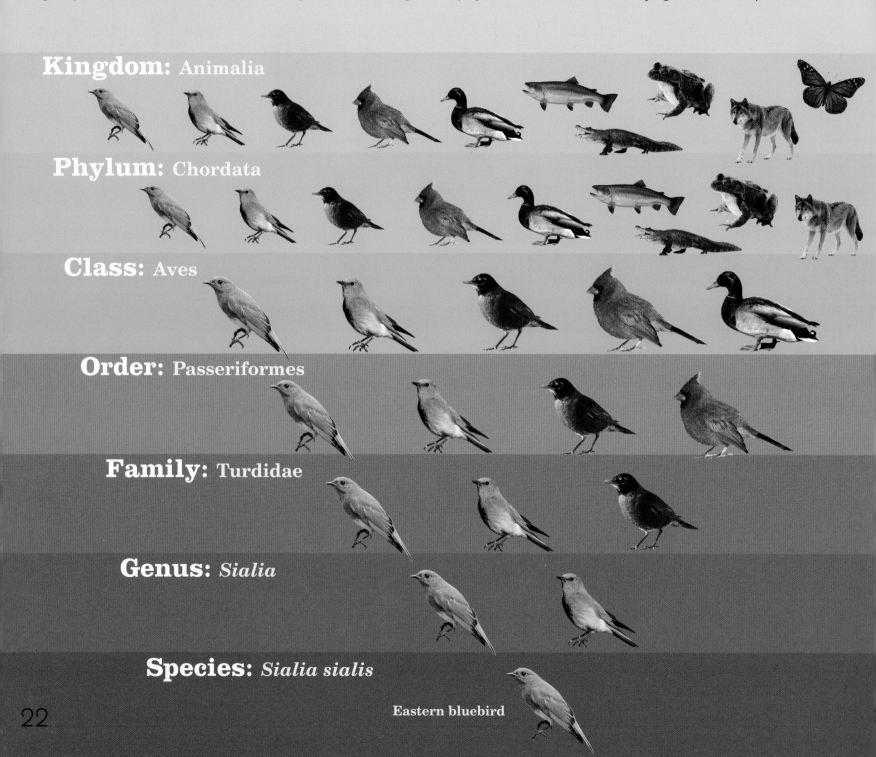

Kingdom: Animalia

Phylum: Chordata

Class: Aves

Order: Passeriformes

Family: Turdidae

Genus: *Sialia*

Species: *Sialia sialis*

Eastern bluebird

Extreme Birds

Smallest bird: The bee hummingbird is the smallest bird in the world. This tiny flier is about 2 inches (5.1 centimeters) long and weighs only 0.05 ounces (1.4 grams). That's about the weight of one paper clip.

Largest bird: An ostrich stands higher than the world's tallest basketball player. This huge bird has been known to grow as tall as 9 feet (2.7 meters) tall, making it the largest bird on Earth.

Fastest bird: The peregrine falcon is the fastest bird. It reaches speeds of up to 200 miles (320 km) per hour when it dives.

Longest wingspan: The bird with the longest wingspan is the mighty albatross. Its giant wings can measure up to 11 feet (3.4 m) across.

Farthest traveler: The arctic tern migrates farther than any other bird, about 25,000 miles (40,000 km) each year. This small bird travels from its home in the Arctic Circle to the edge of the Antarctic every winter.

Longest feathers: The crested argus pheasant loves to show off its grand tail. An adult male has tail feathers that grow as long as 6 feet (1.8 m)—the longest feathers in the world!

Glossary

birds—animals that have feathers and wings, a backbone, lightweight bones, and a four-chambered heart; they are also warm-blooded, and hatch from eggs

habitat—the place and natural conditions in which a plant or animal lives

hover—to stay in one place while flying in the air

invertebrate—an animal without a backbone

lungs—the organs in the chest that help some animals breathe

mate—to join together to produce young

migrate—to move from one place to another

oxygen—a gas that people and animals must breathe to stay alive

predator—an animal that hunts and kills other animals for food

preen—to clean feathers with a beak

prey—an animal that is hunted and eaten for food

scavenger—an animal that feeds on animals that are already dead

skeleton—the bones that support an animal's body

vertebrate—an animal that has a backbone

warm-blooded—having a body temperature that remains the same

webbed feet—feet with wide flaps of skin between the toes

To Learn More

More Books to Read

Pyers, Greg. *Why Am I a Bird?* Chicago: Raintree, 2006.

Richardson, Adele. *Birds*. Mankato, Minn.: Capstone Press, 2005.

Solway, Andrew. *Classifying Birds*. Chicago: Heinemann Library, 2003.

Internet Sites

FactHound offers a safe, fun way to find Internet sites related to this book. All of the sites on FactHound have been researched by our staff.

Here's all you do:

Visit *www.facthound.com*

FactHound will fetch the best sites for you!

Index

Look for all of the books in the Amazing Science: Animal Classification series:

Amphibians: Water-to-Land Animals

Birds: Winged and Feathered Animals

Fish: Finned and Gilled Animals

Insects: Six-Legged Animals

Mammals: Hairy, Milk-Making Animals

Reptiles: Scaly-Skinned Animals